EASIEST KEYBOARD COLLECTION

The Best-Known Advertising Themes

WISE PUBLICATIONS
London/New York/Paris/Sydney/Copenhagen/Madrid

Exclusive Distributors:

Music Sales Limited
8/9 Frith Street,
London W1V 5TZ, England.

Music Sales Pty Limited
120 Rothschild Avenue,
Rosebery, NSW 2018,
Australia.

Order No. AM956550
ISBN 0-7119-7754-2
This book © Copyright 1999 by Wise Publications

Book design by Chloë Alexander
Compiled by Nick Crispin
Music arranged by Roger Day
Music processed by Paul Ewers Music Design

Printed in the United Kingdom by
Caligraving Limited, Thetford, Norfolk.

Cover photograph (Stella Artois) courtesy of Lowe Howard-Spink

Your Guarantee of Quality
As publishers, we strive to produce every book to the highest
commercial standards.
The music has been freshly engraved and the book has been carefully
designed to minimise awkward page turns and to make playing from
it a real pleasure.
Particular care has been given to specifying acid-free, neutral-sized
paper made from pulps which have not been elemental chlorine
bleached. This pulp is from farmed sustainable forests and was
produced with special regard for the environment.
Throughout, the printing and binding have been planned to ensure
a sturdy, attractive publication which should give years of enjoyment.
If your copy fails to meet our high standards, please inform us and
we will gladly replace it.

Music Sales' complete catalogue describes thousands of titles
and is available in full colour sections by subject, direct from
Music Sales Limited. Please state your areas of interest and send a
cheque/postal order for £1.50 for postage to: Music Sales Limited,
Newmarket Road, Bury St. Edmunds, Suffolk IP33 3YB.

www.internetmusicshop.com

Contents

BORN TO BE WILD
(Ford Cougar)

Words & Music by Mars Bonfire
© Copyright 1968 Manitou Music, USA.
MCA Music Limited, 77 Fulham Palace Road, London W6.
All Rights Reserved. International Copyright Secured.

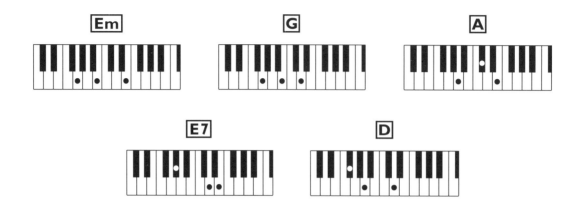

Voice: **Distortion Guitar**

Rhythm: **Rock**

Tempo: ♩ = 140

Get your mo - tor run - ning,___ head out on the high - way.

Look - ing for ad - ven - ture, in what -

- ev - er comes our way._____ Yeah, darl - in' gon - na

make it hap - pen, take the world in a love em - brace.___

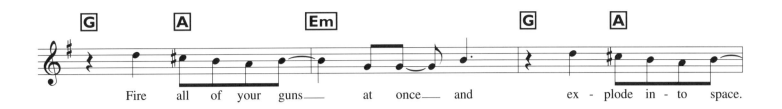

Fire all of your guns at once and ex-plode in-to space.

Like a true na-ture's child, we were

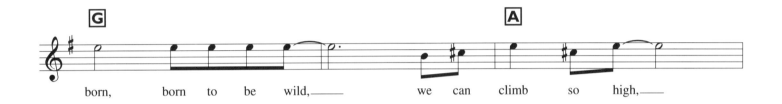

born, born to be wild, we can climb so high,

I nev-er want to die.

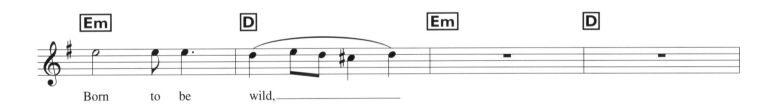

Born to be wild,

born to be wild.

Repeat to fade

CALL ME
(B.T.)

Words & Music by Tony Hatch

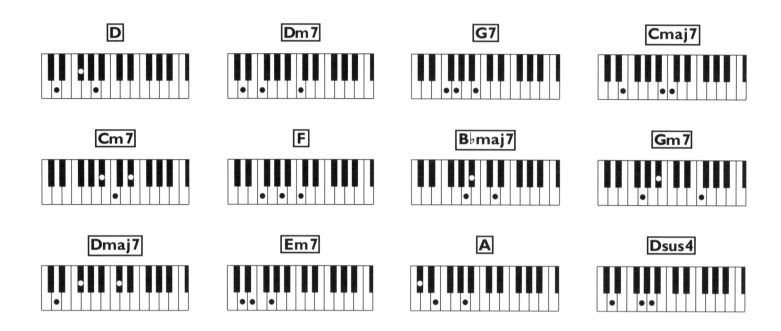

Voice: **Piano**

Rhythm: **Ska**

Tempo: ♩ = 126

If you're feel-ing sad___ and lone-ly, there's a ser-vice I___ can ren - der,

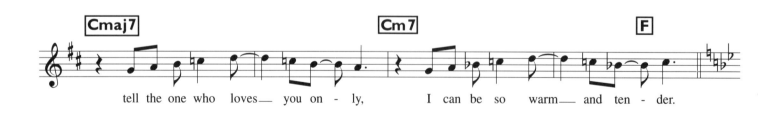

tell the one who loves___ you on - ly, I can be so warm___ and ten - der.

Call me, don't be a - fraid,___ you can call me, may - be it's late,___ but just

call me, tell me and I'll be a - round. Now don't for -

- get me 'cause if you let me I will al - ways stay by you, you've got to

trust me, that's how it must be, there's so much that I can do.

If you call I'll be right with you, you and I should be to - geth - er,

with this love I long to give you, I'll be at your side for - ev - er.

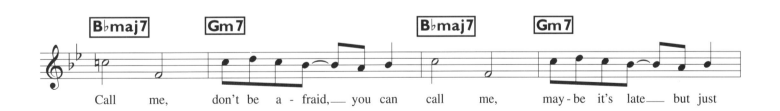

Call me, don't be a - fraid, you can call me, may - be it's late but just

Repeat to fade

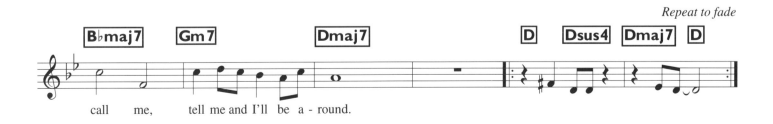

call me, tell me and I'll be a - round.

7

CAN'T TAKE MY EYES OFF YOU

(Peugeot 306/Tennents)

Words & Music by Bob Crewe & Bob Gaudio

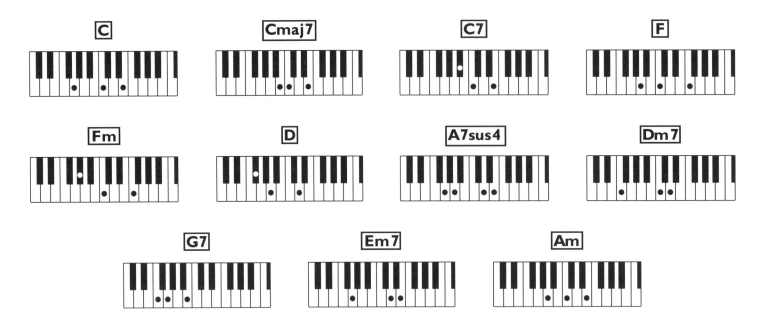

Voice: **Acoustic Guitar**

Rhythm: **Pop Ballad**

Tempo: ♩ = 120

You're just too good to be true,⸺ can't take my

eyes off of you,⸺ you'd be like hea - ven to touch,⸺

⸺ I wan - na hold you so much.⸺ At long last

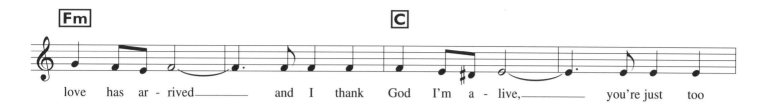

Fm / C

love has ar - rived_____ and I thank God I'm a - live,_____ you're just too

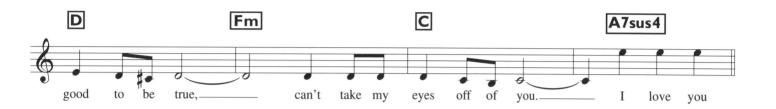

D / Fm / C / A7sus4

good to be true,_____ can't take my eyes off of you._____ I love you

Dm7 / G7 / Em7

ba - by_____ and if it's quite al - right,_____ I need you ba - by,_____ to warm the

Am / Dm7 / G7 / Cmaj7

lone - ly night,_____ I love you ba - by,_____ trust in me_____ when I say,_____

A7sus4 Dm7 / G7

_____ oh pret - ty ba - by,_____ don't bring me down I pray,_____ oh pret - ty

Em7 / Am / Dm7

ba - by_____ now that I've found you, stay_____ and let me love you,_____ ba -

G7 / Cmaj7

- by, let me love you._____

CUM ON FEEL THE NOIZE
(Fiat Seicento)

Words & Music by Jim Lea & Noddy Holder

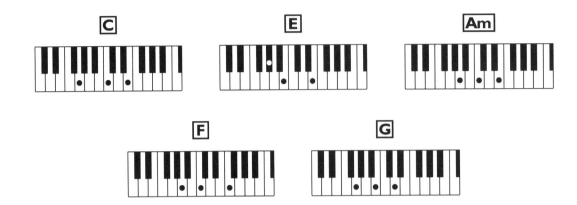

Voice: **Electric Guitar**

Rhythm: **Rock**

Tempo: ♩ = 136

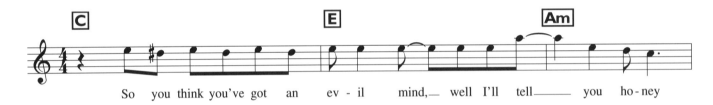

So you think you've got an ev-il mind,— well I'll tell—— you ho-ney

and I don't know why,—— and I don't know why.

—— So you think my sing-ing's out of time,— well it makes

—— me mo-ney, and I don't know why—— and I

FEMALE OF THE SPECIES
(Impulse)

Words & Music by Tommy Scott, James Edwards, Francis Griffiths & Andrew Parle

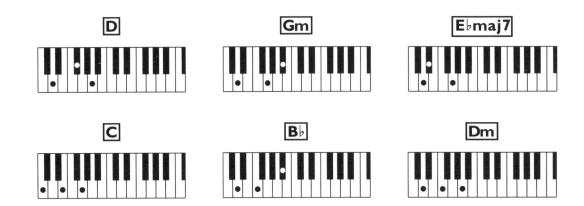

Voice: **Distortion Guitar**

Rhythm: **8 Beat Pop**

Tempo: ♩ = 112

A thou-sand thun-der-ing thrills a-wait___ me,

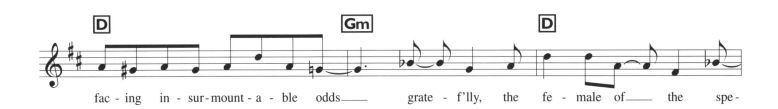

fac-ing in-sur-mount-a-ble odds___ grate-f'lly, the fe-male of___ the spe-

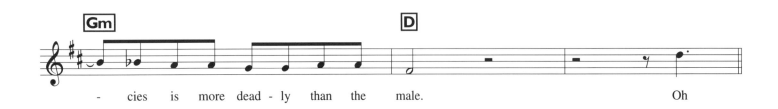

-cies is more dead-ly than the male.   Oh

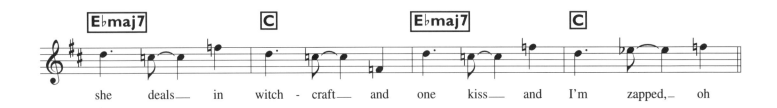

she deals___ in witch-craft___ and one kiss___ and I'm zapped,___ oh

how can hea - ven hold a place for me, when — a girl like you has cast a spell on

me, oh, — how can hea - ven hold a place for me when — a

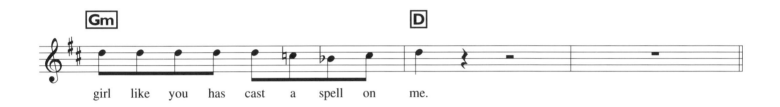

girl like you has cast a spell on me.

Oh —

how can hea - ven hold a place for me, when — a girl like you has cast a spell on

me, oh, — how can hea - ven hold a place for me when — a

girl like you has cast a spell on me.

FLOWER DUET (from 'Lakmé')
(British Airways)

Composed by Léo Delibes

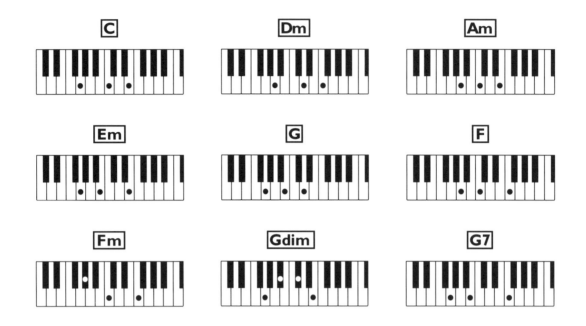

Voice: **Flute**

Rhythm: **Waltz**

Tempo: ♩ = 132

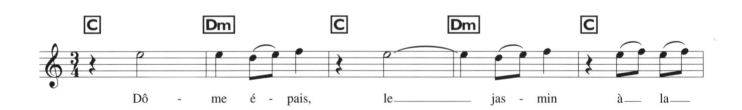

Dô - me é - pais, le____ jas - min à la____

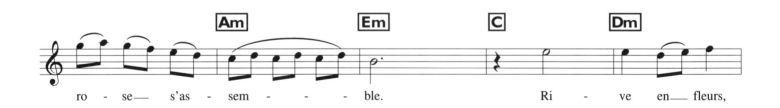

ro - se____ s'as - sem - - ble. Ri - ve en____ fleurs,

frais_____ ma - tin, nous__ ap - pel - lent__ en - sem - - ble.

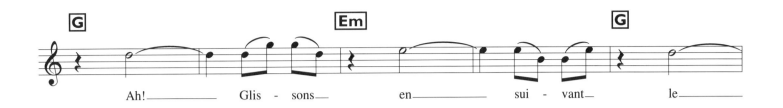

Ah!_____ Glis - sons_____ en_____ sui - vant_____ le_____

_____ cou - rant_____ fu - yant,_____ dans_____ l'on - - - -

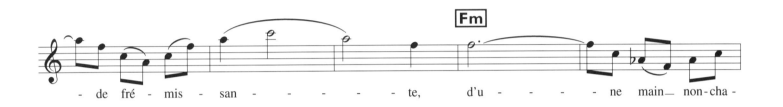

- de fré - mis - san - - - - - te, d'u - - - ne main non - cha -

- lan - - - - - te, ga - - - gnons_____ le bord,

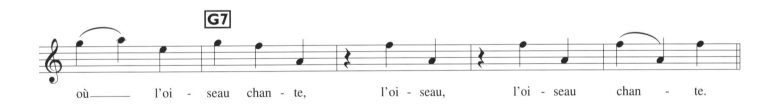

où_____ l'oi - seau chan - te, l'oi - seau, l'oi - seau chan - te.

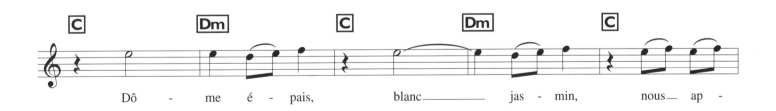

Dô - me é - pais, blanc_____ jas - min, nous_____ ap -

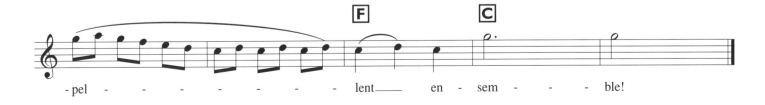

-pel - - - - - - - lent_____ en - sem - - - ble!

FLY AWAY

(Peugeot 206)

Words & Music by Lenny Kravitz
© Copyright 1998 Miss Bessie Music, USA.
EMI Virgin Music Limited, 127 Charing Cross Road, London WC2.
All Rights Reserved. International Copyright Secured.

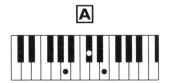   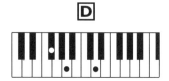

Voice: **String/Piano Split**

Rhythm: **Funky Pop 1**

Tempo: ♩= 142

I wish that I could fly in -

-to the sky, so ve - ry high, just like a

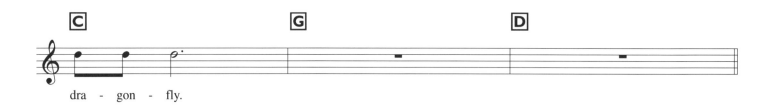

dra - gon - fly.

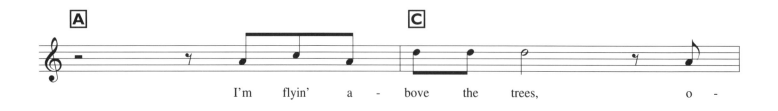

I'm flyin' a - bove the trees, o -

-ver the seas in all de - grees, to_____ a - ny -

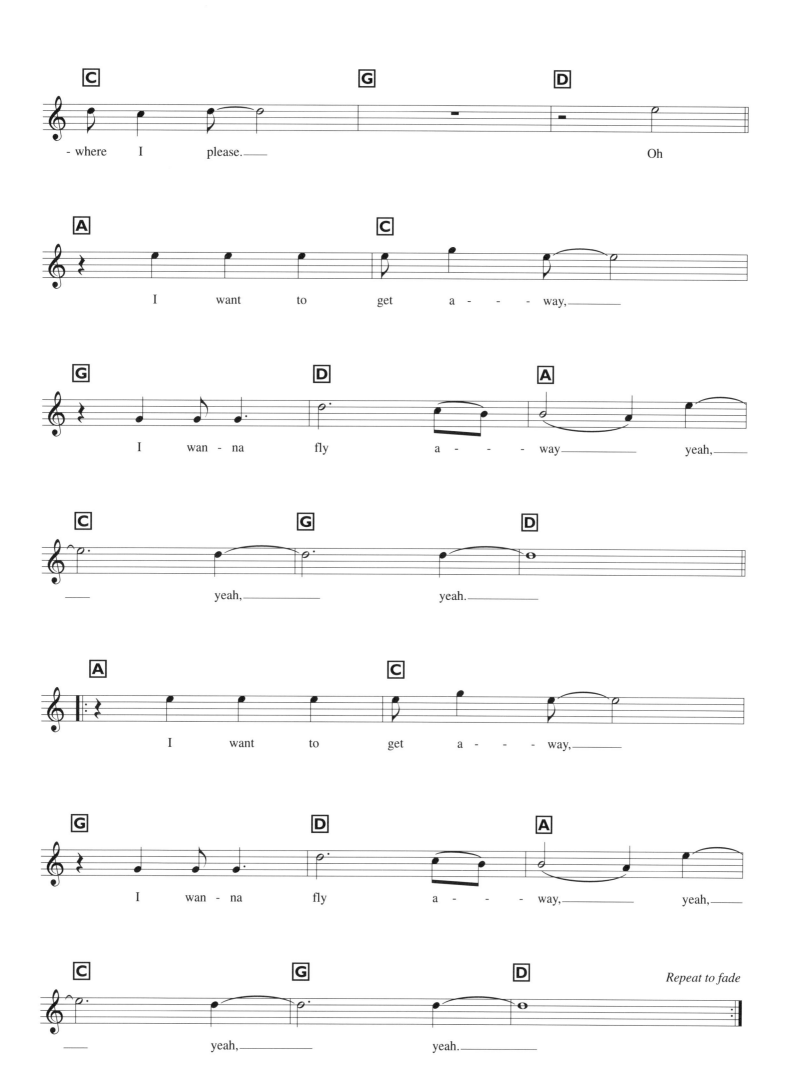

GET DOWN TONIGHT
(Budweiser Bud Ice)

Words & Music by Harry Casey & Richard Finch
© Copyright 1974 Longitude Music Company, USA.
Peermusic (UK) Limited, 8-14 Verulam Street, London WC1.
All Rights Reserved. International Copyright Secured

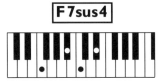

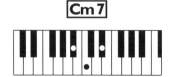
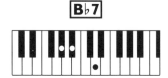

Voice: **Synth Bass**

Rhythm: **Dance Pop 1**

Tempo: ♩ = 116

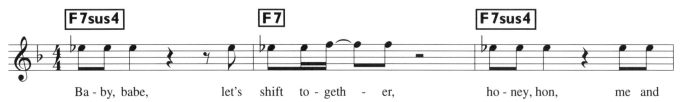

Ba - by, babe, let's shift to - geth - er, ho - ney, hon, me and

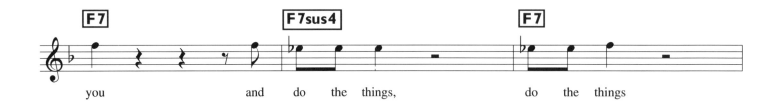

you and do the things, do the things

that we___ like to do. Do a lit - tle dance, make a lit - tle love, get

down to - night,___ get down to - night.___ Do a lit - tle dance,

make a lit - tle love, get down to - night,___ get down to - night.___

Ba - by, babe, I need you. Same place, same time.—

— Well we can al - ways get to - geth - er and

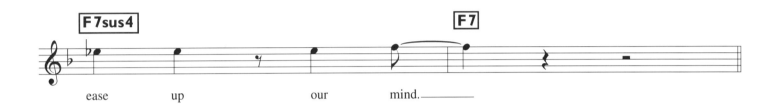

ease up our mind.—

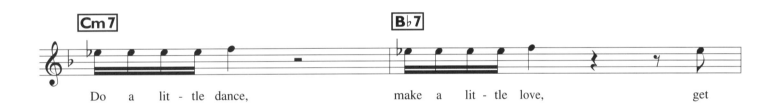

Do a lit - tle dance, make a lit - tle love, get

down to - night,— get down to - night.— Do a lit - tle dance,

make a lit - tle love, get down to - night,— get down to - night.—

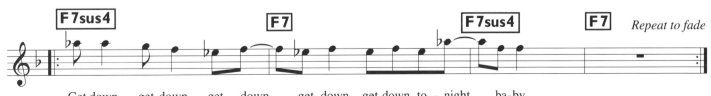

Repeat to fade

Get down, get down, get down,— get down, get down to - night— ba - by.

GUAGLIONE
(Guinness)

By Giovanni Fanciulli & Nisa
© Copyright 1956 renewed 1984 by Accordo Edizioni Musicali, Milan.
Controlled for the UK, Eire, Australia & New Zealand by Eaton Music Limited, 8 West Eaton Place, London SW1X 8LS.
All Rights Reserved. International Copyright Secured.

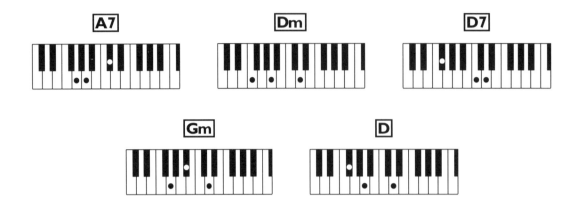

Voice: **Electric Organ 3**

Rhythm: **Cha Cha**

Tempo: ♩= 140

I JUST WANT TO MAKE LOVE TO YOU
(Diet Coke)

Words & Music by Willie Dixon

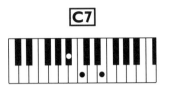 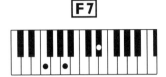 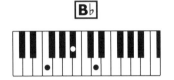 

Voice: **Piano 1**

Rhythm: **16 Beat Shuffle**

Tempo: ♩ = 108

I don't want you to be no slave, I don't want you

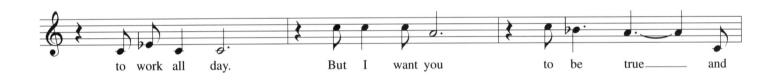

to work all day. But I want you to be true___ and

I just want to make love___ to you. Love___ to you,

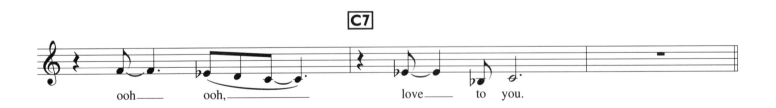

ooh___ ooh,___ love___ to you.

All I want to do is wash your clothes, I don't want to

keep you in-doors. There is no-thing for you to do—— but

keep me mak - ing love—— to you. Love —— to you,

ooh—— ooh,———— love—— to you. And I can

tell by the way you walk that walk, and I can hear by the way you

talk that talk, and I can know by the way you treat your girl that I could

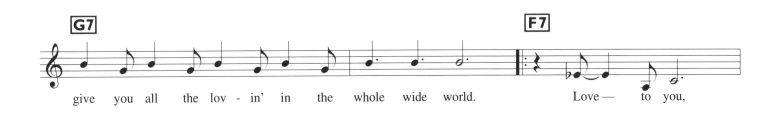

give you all the lov - in' in the whole wide world. Love —— to you,

Repeat to fade

ooh—— ooh,———— love—— to you.

JEAN DE FLORETTE (Theme)
(Stella Artois)

Words & Music by Jean-Claude Petit
© Copyright Renn Productions SARL, France/SDRM.
All Rights Reserved. International Copyright Secured.

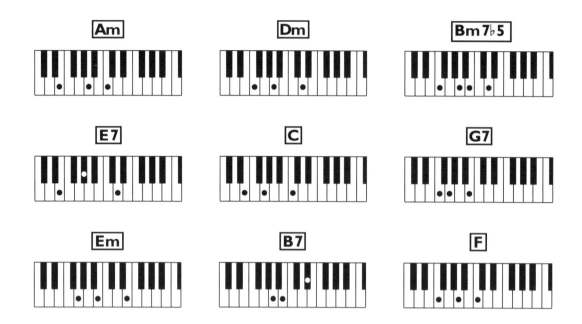

Voice: **Clarinet**

Rhythm: **Serenade**

Tempo: ♩= **98**

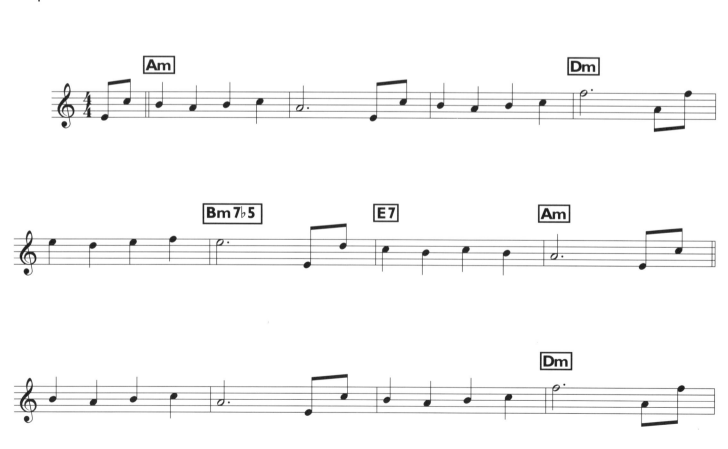

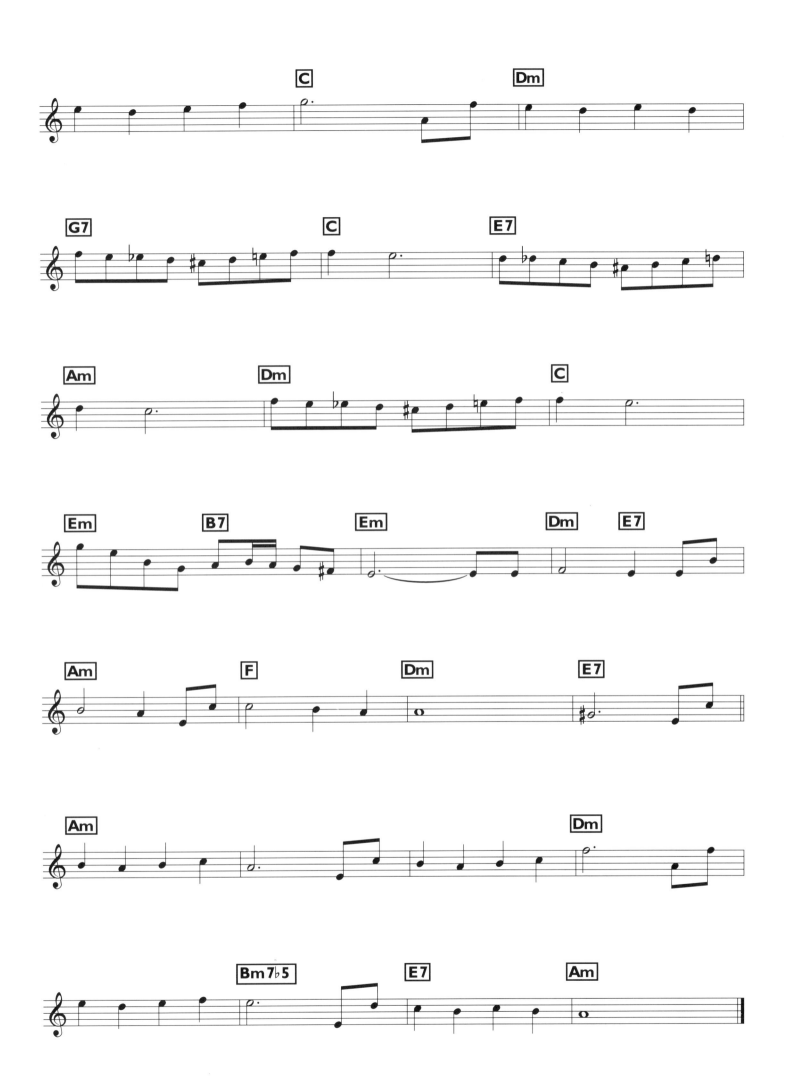

JOHNNY AND MARY
(Renault)

Words & Music by Robert Palmer

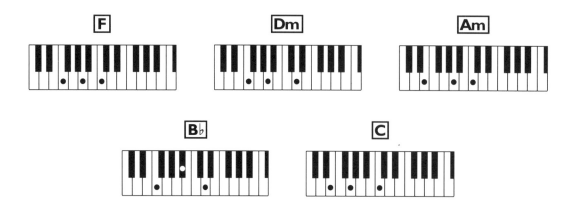

Voice: **Jazz Guitar**

Rhythm: **Cool**

Tempo: ♩ = 144

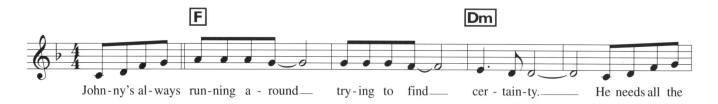

John-ny's al-ways run-ning a-round___ try-ing to find___ cer-tain-ty.___ He needs all the

world to con-firm___ that he ain't lone - ly. Ma-ry counts the

walls,___ knows he ti-res ea - si-ly.___ John-ny thinks the

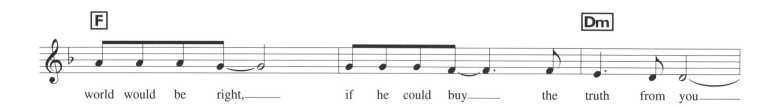

world would be right,___ if he could buy___ the truth from you

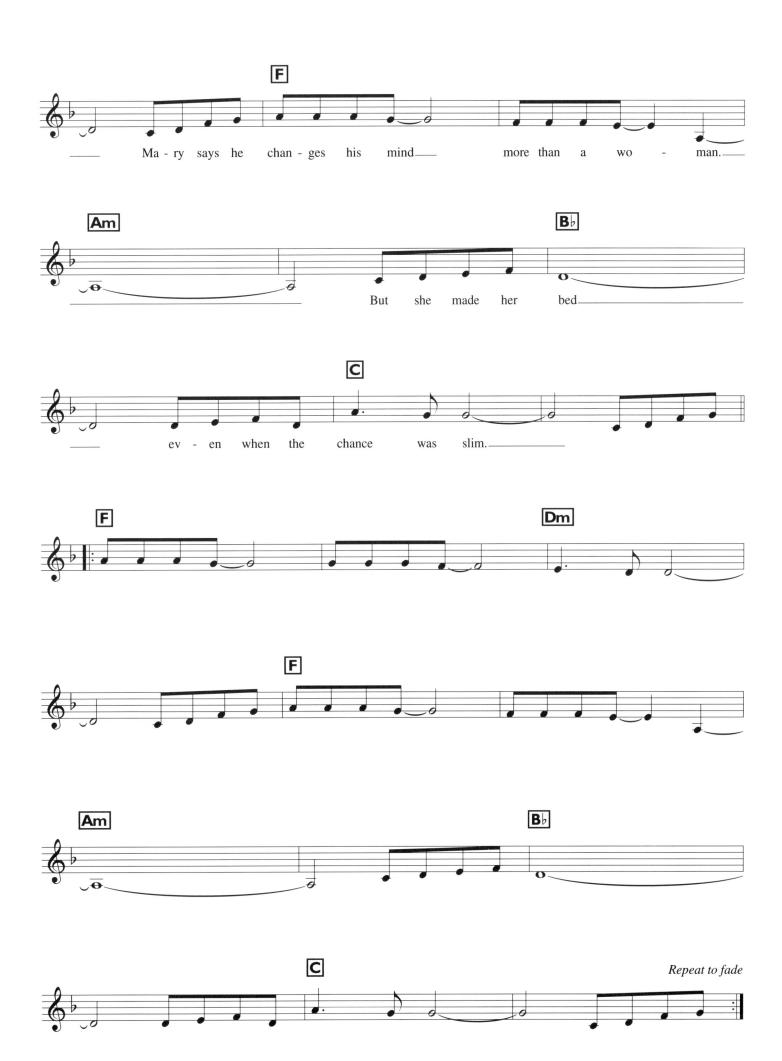

Ma - ry says he chan - ges his mind⏜ more than a wo - man.

But she made her bed⏜

⏜ ev - en when the chance was slim.⏜

Repeat to fade

JUMP, JIVE AN' WAIL
(GAP Jeans)

Words & Music by Louis Prima

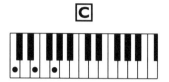 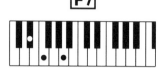 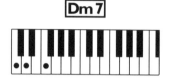 

Voice: **Honky-tonk Piano**

Rhythm: **50s Rock 'n' Roll**

Tempo: ♩= 160

Ba - by, ba - by it looks like it's gon - na hail.

Ba - by, ba - by it looks like it's gon - na hail. You'd bet - ter

come in - side, let me teach you how to jive and wail. You got - ta

jump and jive and then you wail. You got - ta jump and jive and then you wail. You got - ta

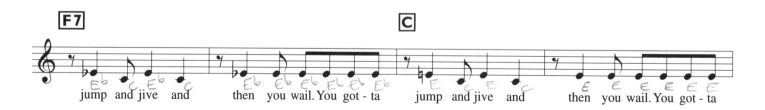

jump and jive and then you wail. You got - ta jump and jive and then you wail. You got - ta

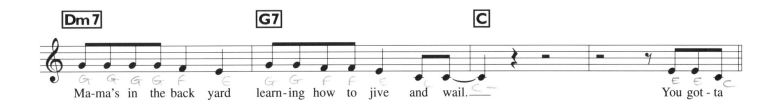

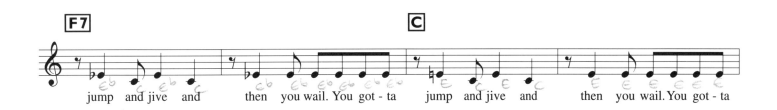

MAGIC MOMENTS
(Quality Street)

Words & Music by Burt Bacharach & Hal David
© Copyright 1957 Casa David Music Incorporated & Famous Music Corporation, (50%), USA.
MCA Music Limited, 77 Fulham Palace Road, London W6 (50%).
All Rights Reserved. International Copyright Secured.

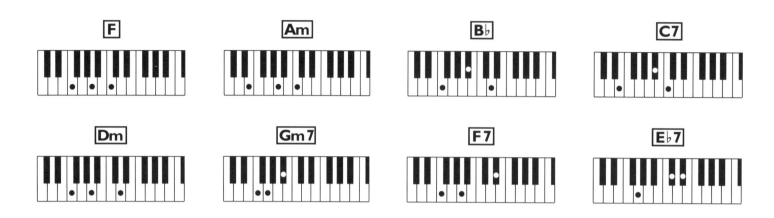

Voice: **Piano**

Rhythm: **Love Ballad**

Tempo: ♩. = 96

I'll nev - er for - get the mo - ment we

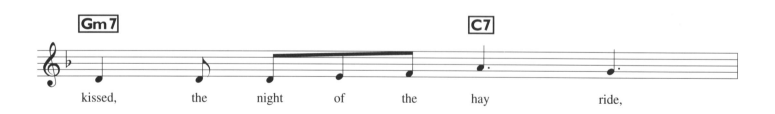

kissed, the night of the hay ride,

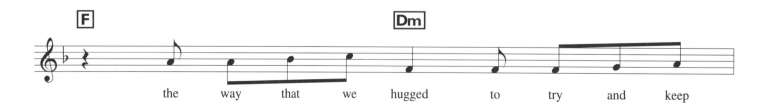

the way that we hugged to try and keep

MARVELLOUS
(Renault Megane Scenic)

Words & Music by Ian Broudie

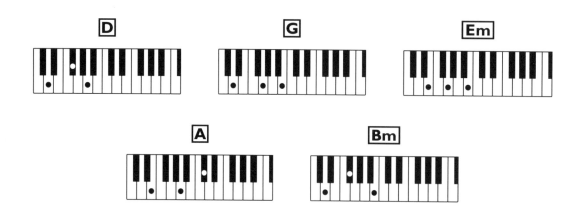

Voice: **Electric Piano 1**

Rhythm: **Soft Rock 1**

Tempo: ♩ = 132

Oh— you hope to fit but you're fit to drop, o-pen up the win-dow and jump

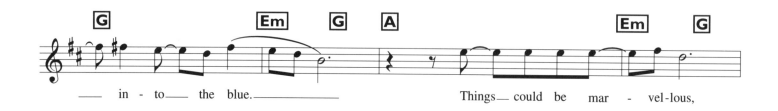

—— in - to—— the blue.———— Things— could be mar - vel-lous,

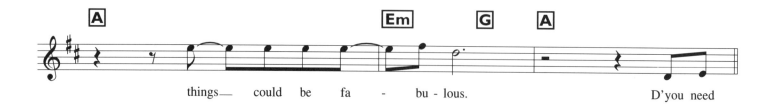

things— could be fa - bu - lous. D'you need

a push, I'll push—— you off, o-pen up the win-dow and jump—

_____ in - to _____ the blue._____ Things_ could be mar - vel-lous soon._____

Oh, well these are the days_____ and this is the life,_____ there'll al-ways be some - thing on_____ your mind,

_____ you'll nev - er quite find, won't you ev - er make_____ your mind_____ up?

Now you'll nev - er be sure,_____ if this is the time,_____ if this is the mo -

- ment, the end of the line,_____ you'll nev - er de - cide, you used to know_____ but now_____

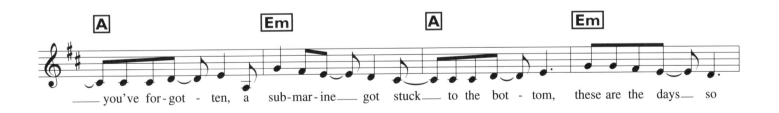

_____ you've for - got - ten, a sub - mar - ine_____ got stuck_____ to the bot - tom, these are the days_____ so

wake up, 'cause this is the time,_____ and you know_____ I'm right.

PATRICIA
(Royal Mail)

Music by Perez Prado
English Lyric by Bob Marcus

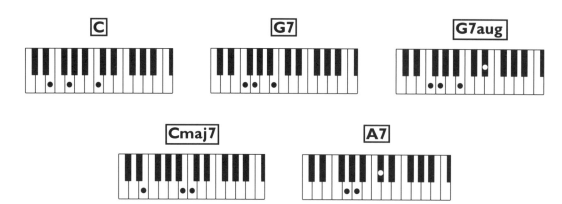

Voice: **Trumpet**

Rhythm: **Mambo**

Tempo: ♩ = 122

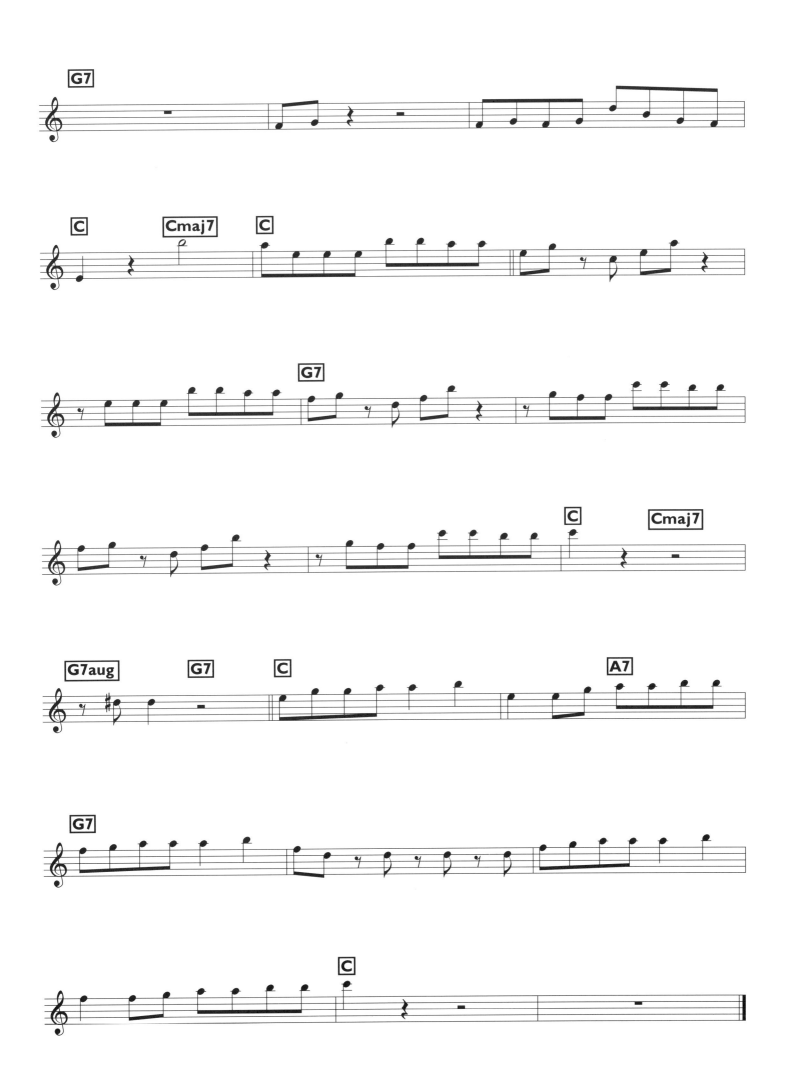

SEARCH FOR THE HERO
(Peugeot 406)

Words & Music by Mike Pickering & Paul Heard

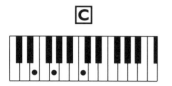 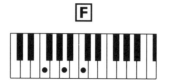  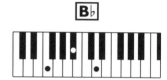

Voice: **Clarinet**

Rhythm: **8 Beat Pop**

Tempo: ♩ = 116

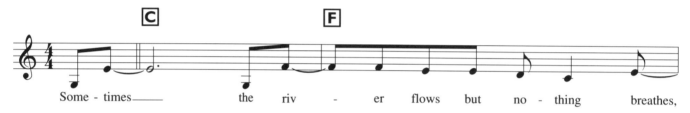

Some - times____ the riv - er flows but no - thing breathes,

____ a train____ ar - rives but____ nev - er leaves,____ it's a

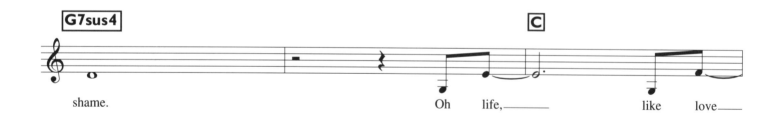

shame. Oh life,____ like love____

____ that walks out of the door,____ of be - ing rich or____ be - ing poor,—

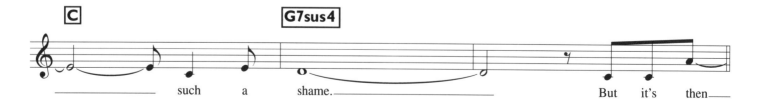

____ such a shame.____ But it's then____

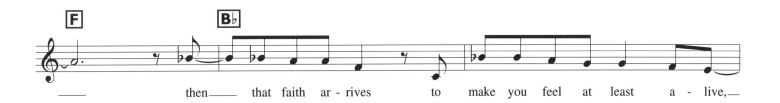

then——— that faith ar - rives to make you feel at least a - live,———

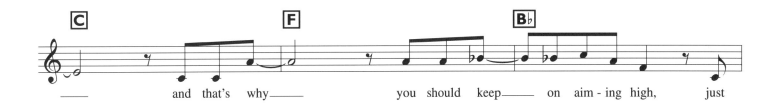

and that's why——— you should keep——— on aim - ing high, just

seek your - self and you will find.——— You've got to

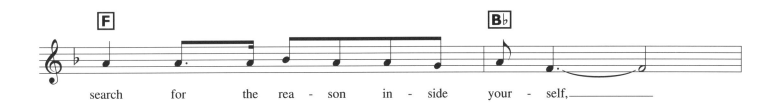

search for the rea - son in - side your - self,———

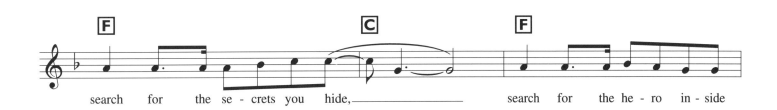

search for the se - crets you hide,——— search for the he - ro in - side

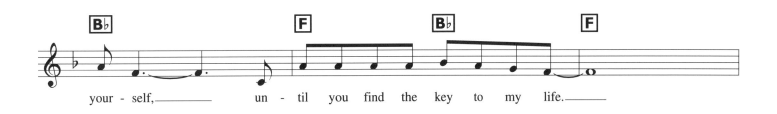

your - self,——— un - til you find the key to my life.———

SHE'S A LADY
(Weetabix)

Words & Music by Paul Anka

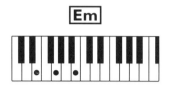
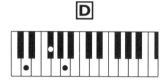
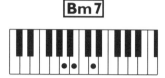

Voice: **Soprano Saxophone**

Rhythm: **Soft Rock 2**

Tempo: ♩ = 116

Well she's all you'd ev-er want, she's the kind men like to flaunt and take to

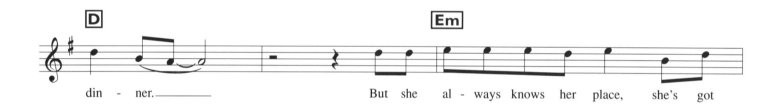

din - ner._____ But she al - ways knows her place, she's got

style, she's got grace, she's a win - ner._____ She's a

la - dy. Woh,_ woh,_ woh, she's a la - dy._____ Talk-in' a - bout_ that lit - tle

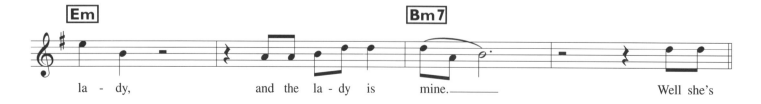

la - dy, and the la - dy is mine._____ Well she's

nev - er in the way, al - ways some - thing nice to say, what a

bless - ing. I can leave her on her own, know - ing

she's O. K. a - lone, she's a la - dy. She's a

la - dy. Woh, woh, woh, she's a la - dy.

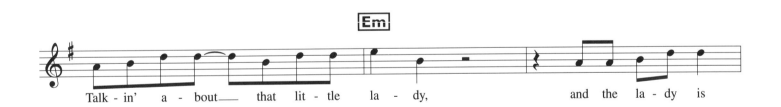

Talk - in' a - bout that lit - tle la - dy, and the la - dy is

mine, yeah, yeah. She's a la - dy, woh,

Repeat to fade

woh, woh, she's a la - dy, lis - ten to me now. She's a

SPEAKING OF HAPPINESS
(Ford Mondeo)

Words & Music by Jimmy Radcliffe & Buddy Scott

© Copyright 1966 Vogue Music, USA.
PolyGram Music Publishing Limited, 47 British Grove, London W4.

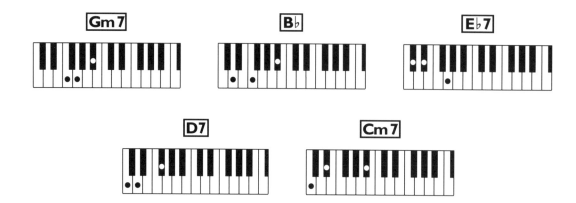

Voice: **Trumpet**

Rhythm: **Big Band**

Tempo: = 108

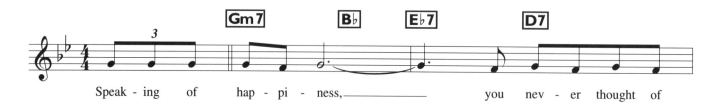

Speak - ing of hap - pi - ness,_____ you nev - er thought of

mine._____ Men - tion - ing the lone - li - ness,

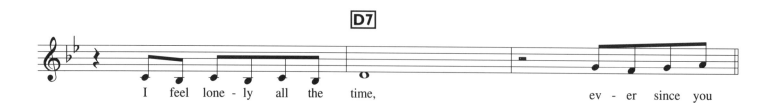

I feel lone - ly all the time, ev - er since you

went a - way af - ter swear - ing we would nev - er part,

there was no-thing I could say, who could talk with a bro-ken

heart. Speak - ing of hap - pi - ness

why did it have to leave,____ speak - ing of

busi - ness,____ why could-'nt it just leave? I love you so____

____ ve - ry much, how could a - ny - thing real - ly go wrong,

Repeat to fade

with the ma - gic of your touch and your love to keep me

strong.____

THE STORY OF MY LIFE
(Guinness)

Music by Burt Bacharach
Words by Hal David

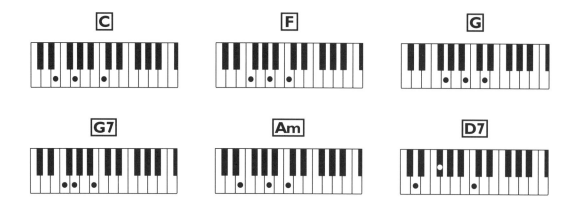

Voice: **Flute**

Rhythm: **Love Ballad**

Tempo: ♩ = 134

Some - day I'm gon - na write the sto - ry of my

life, I'll tell a - bout the night we met and how my heart

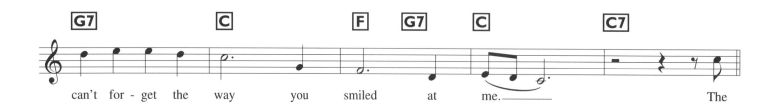

can't for - get the way you smiled at me. The

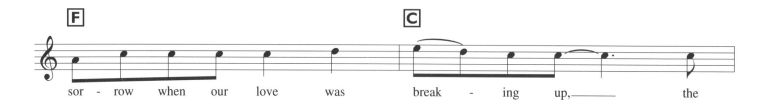

sor - row when our love was break - ing up, the

THEME FROM E.T. (The Extra-Terrestrial)
(B.T.)

By John Williams

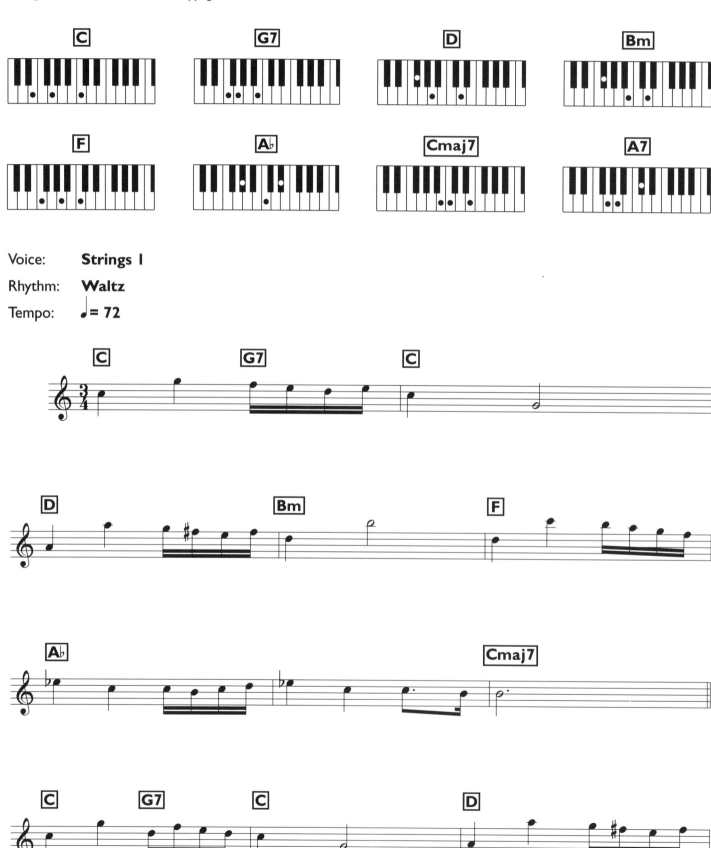

Voice: **Strings 1**

Rhythm: **Waltz**

Tempo: ♩ = 72

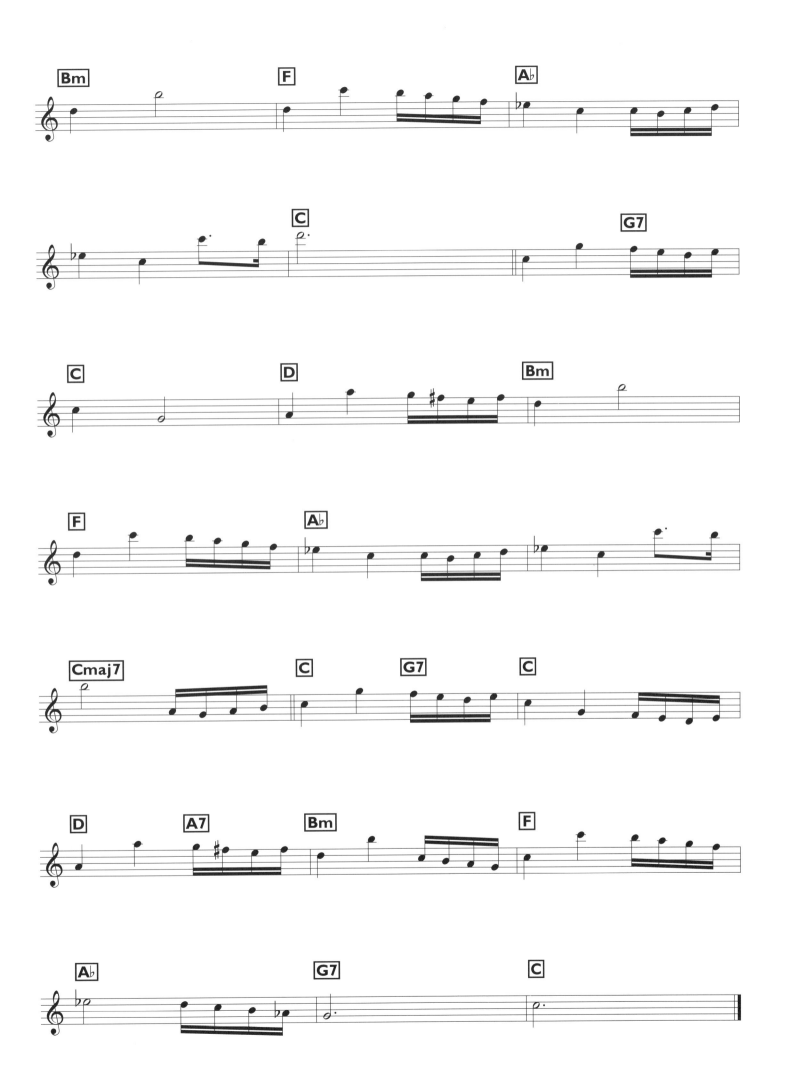

YOU GOTTA BE
(Ford Focus)

Lyrics & Melody by Des'ree
Music by Ashley Ingram

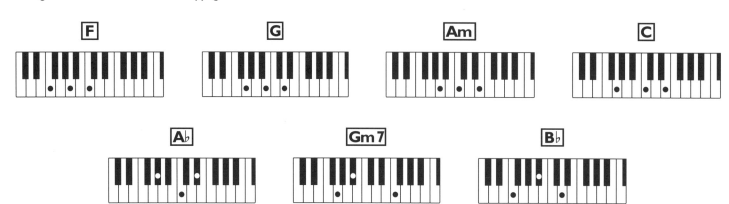

Voice: **Piano**

Rhythm: **Groove Soul**

Tempo: ♩ = 92

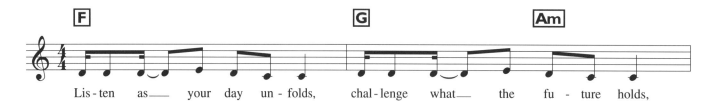

Lis-ten as— your day un-folds, chal-lenge what— the fu-ture holds,

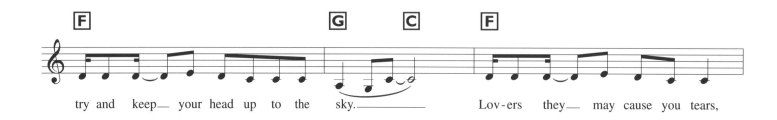

try and keep— your head up to the sky.— Lov-ers they— may cause you tears,

go a-head,— re-lease your fears, stand up and be count-ed, don't be 'shamed to cry.— You got-ta be,

you got-ta be bad, you got-ta be bold, you got-ta be wis-er, you got-ta be hard, you got-ta be

EASIEST KEYBOARD COLLECTION

Easy-to-play melody line arrangements for all keyboards with chord symbols and lyrics. Suggested registration, rhythm and tempo are included for each song together with keyboard diagrams showing left-hand chord voicings used.

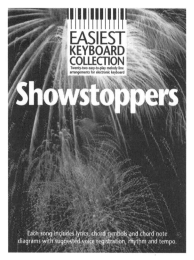

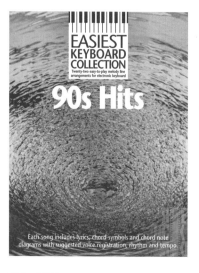

Showstoppers

Consider Yourself (Oliver!), Do You Hear The People Sing? (Les Misérables), I Know Him So Well (Chess), Maria (West Side Story), Smoke Gets In Your Eyes (Roberta) and 17 more big stage hits.
Order No. AM944218

Pop Classics

A Whiter Shade Of Pale (Procol Harum), Bridge Over Troubled Water (Simon & Garfunkel), Crocodile Rock (Elton John) and nineteen more classic pop hits, including Hey Jude (The Beatles), Imagine (John Lennon), Massachusetts (The Bee Gees) and Stars (Simply Red).
Order No. AM944196

90s Hits

Over twenty of the greatest hits of the 1990s, including Always (Bon Jovi), Fields Of Gold (Sting), Have I Told You Lately (Rod Stewart), One Sweet Day (Mariah Carey), Say You'll Be There (Spice Girls), and Wonderwall (Oasis).
Order No. AM944229

TV Themes

Twenty-two great themes from popular TV series, including Casualty, EastEnders, Gladiators, Heartbeat, I'm Always Here (Baywatch), Red Dwarf and The Black Adder.
Order No. AM944207

Also available...

Ballads, Order No. AM952116 **Film Themes**, Order No. AM952050
Boyzone, Order No. AM958331 **Hits of the 90s**, Order No. AM955780
Broadway, Order No. AM952127 **Jazz Classics**, Order No. AM952061
Chart Hits, Order No. AM952083 **Love Songs**, Order No. AM950708
Christmas, Order No. AM952105 **Pop Hits**, Order No. AM952072
Classic Blues, Order No. AM950697 **60s Hits**, Order No. AM955768
Classical Themes, Order No. AM952094 **80s Hits**, Order No. AM955779